Pursue Confidently

A Guide to Embrace Your Value and Pursue Your Goals

Latasha G. Hines, Esq.

Jewel Publishers

Jewel Publishers, LLC
P.O. Box 278006
Miramar, Florida 33027
www.jewelpublishers.com

In accordance with the U.S. Copyright Act of 1976, the contents and cover of this book may not be reproduced or transmitted in any form or by any means, electronically or mechanically, except within the fair use laws, without written permission from the author. To request written permission to reproduce copies of portions of this book, write to: Latasha Gethers Hines, P.O. Box 278006, Miramar, FL 33027, latashahines@jewelpublishers.com.

Pursue Confidently
A Guide to Embrace Your Value
and Pursue Your Goals

Copyright© 2015 Latasha Gethers Hines

Jewel Publishers, LLC
P.O. Box 278006
Miramar, Florida 33027
www.jewelpublishers.com

ISBN-13: 978-0-9778322-9-3

Author's Cover Photo by K. Sheree
Printed in the United States of America

Dedications

I dedicate *Pursue Confidently* to my daughter, Mikayla Michelle Hines, and my son, Matthew Aaron Hines. You are precious gifts from the Creator. I pray that you will journey through this life with confidence as you pursue your goals. Love yourself. Love others. And, know that you are worthy to be loved.

To my nieces, Ryan Porter and Zuri Porter, I dedicate this book to you. You are precious indeed. Know that I love you dearly.

Acknowledgements

I honor my triune God—God the Father; God the Son, Jesus Christ; and God the Holy Spirit—for empowering me to pursue confidently.

I honor my husband, Travis Hines. Thank you for helping me confidently pursue my dreams.

My dear sister-friend, Valerie Lively, thank you for 30 years of treasured friendship and your assistance with this manuscript.

I acknowledge my fellow attorney, professional speaker, and author, Asiah Wolfolk-Manning, Esq. Thank you for being a loving, supportive, and skilled "midwife" who empowered me to birth *Pursue Confidently*. You are a gift.

Contents

	Introduction	7
	Instructions	9

Session	**Part I – Be Confident; Love Yourself**	
1	You Are the Designer's Original	13
2	You Are a Gift	19
3	You Are Equipped	25
4	Activate Your Plan	31

Part II – Be Confident; Embrace Healthy Relationships

5	Created to Love Others	35
6	Worthy to Be Loved	41
7	Love Confidently	47
8	Activate Your Plan	53

Contents Continued

Part III – Be Confident; Pursue Your Goals

9	Purse with Urgency............................	57
10	Pursue with Excellence......................	63
11	Pursue Confidently............................	69
12	Activate Your Plan............................	75
	Closing..	77

Introduction

To pursue is "to find or employ measures to obtain or accomplish." (*Merriam-Webster*. Web. 02 Apr. 2015.) Confidence is "the feeling of being certain that something will happen or that something is true." (Ibid.)

You must begin the pursuit because there are some things you must accomplish. The desire to accomplish certain goals burns within you. While the flames may become dull over time as discouragement, busyness, and fear try to overtake you, the flame still burns. What must you accomplish before you leave this earth? What blessing must you share with the world?

Whatever "it" is, you must pursue. You must employ measures to accomplish that goal. You have already employed some measures to accomplish that goal. You have thought about it, prayed about it, or talked to someone about your idea. Even if it is just a thought, the pursuit is underway; you are out of the starting block. Now it is time to take the necessary actions to run the distance to achieve your goal. No matter where you are on the journey, *Pursue Confidently* will help you intensify your pursuit.

Not only will you intensify your pursuit, you will be empowered to pursue with confidence. You will pursue your goal with confidence as you embrace the fact that you are a precious gift with gifts to share with others. Your confidence is established as you embrace the truth that you are a gift to this world. You must love you.

Moreover, as you learn to love others and be loved by others, you will build healthy relationships to help propel you toward your goals. Out of the wellspring of love of oneself flows the ability to love and be loved by others. I do not mean selfish love that leads to pride or self-seeking love that makes one think they are better than others. We need to love ourselves in a way that affirms that we are precious gifts with gifts to share with others.

Our ability to extend and receive love impacts our confidence in pursuing our goals. As we love ourselves, recognizing that we are special gifts to this world, our confidence to pursue our goals is planted. As we love others, sharing the gift of ourselves with others, our confidence to pursue our goals is nourished. As we receive the love of others, enjoying the reciprocity of love returned, our confidence to pursue our goals grows.

Journey Confidently is a guide. You must do the work required to accomplish your goals. Some sessions are designed to lead you to address areas of your life that may interfere with your ability to pursue your goals with confidence. Other sections are designed to empower you to begin pursuing your goals or make advancements in your pursuit. Come on. Let's do it! Let us prepare to embrace *Pursue Confidently*.

Latasha G. Hines, Esq.

Instructions

Pursue Confidently is a 12-section guide to embrace your value and pursue your goals. You will be empowered to love yourself and embrace healthy relationships where love is given and received as you confidently pursue your goals. This book will guide you through written exercises of self-reflection, goal setting, future encouragement, and plan activation.

Pursue Confidently is divided into three parts covering 12 sections. First, meditate on the statements and questions and respond to each. Second, identify a major goal you want to accomplish that is directly related to the topic in each section. You likely have more than one goal. However, as you work through this section of the book the first time, try to focus on one goal.

Third, write a letter to yourself for the future. In this letter, you will acknowledge where you are now in your pursuit, discuss where you hope to be one year from now, and encourage yourself to keep pressing forward to accomplish the identified goal.

At the end of Parts I, II, and III, you will identify precise steps to take to activate your plan to reach your goal. In the goal activation section that follows Parts I, II, and III, consider the principles discussed in the sessions that make up each part. The goal-setting activities are the same for Parts I, II, and III. However, you will find that as you embrace certain principles along the way, you may redefine your goal or strategy. For this reason, the goal-setting activities are worth repeating.

Pursue Confidently may be used as a personal study guide or in a group. Feel free to complete the sections at your own pace. Whether you explore *Pursue Confidently* alone or in a group of trusted friends or associates, I encourage you to dedicate time alone with God to address each section.

When you come together as a group, make a commitment to each other that you will not reveal personal matters discussed within the group to others. Allow each member to share as much or as little as they are comfortable sharing, but encourage each member to share. Sharing your goals and journey among fellow group members will impact the lives of all participants.

Latasha G. Hines, Esq.

Part I

Be Confident; Love Yourself

Many of us are familiar with the mandate to love your neighbor as you love yourself. (Matthew 22:39.) This is an absolute principle established in God's Word. It is a universal principle that compels us to significantly consider the needs of others.

The principle that requires us to love others as we love ourselves suggests that we must in fact love ourselves first. Our neighbor does not benefit if the love we have for ourselves is weak. Our neighbor barely benefits if the love we have for ourselves is mediocre. But encouraging, giving, protective love that begins with oneself greatly benefits our neighbor when we love them as we love ourselves.

Recognize that the Designer took great care in creating you—the Designer's original, His masterpiece. (I reverently refer to God as the "Designer.") (Session 1) Embrace the fact that you are a precious gift, created with purpose, created to be a gift to others. (Session 2)

Love yourself. As you treat yourself with love and respect, you create an environment that suggests to others that they should treat you the same.

Accept that your life's journey thus far has equipped you to pursue your goals. The lessons learned from victories and failures are valuable. Use the lessons you have learned along the way to empower you to pursue your goals. (Session 3)

In this phase of our pursuit, we must embrace self-love as a catalyst to propel us toward pursuing our goals.

Latasha G. Hines, Esq.

Session 1

You Are the Designer's Original

Of the seven billion people on earth, none have the very same qualities as you. You are unique. Your finger print is different than any other individual on this planet. While you may have what appears to be the same complexion as one person, the same eyes as another, the same personality of yet another, or the same talents as someone, there is none quite like you. The Creator of seven billion people (and counting) took care to design a unique masterpiece—you.

Designers of clothes, sculptures, hand bags, shoes, toys, and even common household items like tables, chairs, plates, and even garbage cans take great care in the design process. There is purpose behind every seam placed in the shirt, every angle in the sculpture, the leather in the handbag, the heel on the shoe, the placement of the button on the toy, the rounded edge of the table, the etching on the leg of the chair, the design etched in the plate, and even the lever on the garbage can. Designers take care in creating what they believe will bring pleasure, often first to themselves, then to others.

Pursue Confidently

So it was in the creation of you. Your Designer took great care to design an original person—you. (Psalm 139:14.) Embrace your originality. The Designer took great care to set you apart from the other seven billion people He created. Ignore the doubts that surface to hamper your pursuit of your goals. Stop comparing yourself to others, looking to them to set the standards. Look to your Designer for your purpose, then pursue it. Embrace you. Be you, knowing that the Designer took great care in creating you.

Take the risks of creating and dreaming outside of the box. Today, we have the music of the legendary James Brown who dared to combine the sounds of gospel with R&B, turning it into soul, and then funk music.

What will you—the Designer's original—give this world?

You are the Designer's original. Reflect on the following and write your thoughts.

I am the Designer's original; there is none like me.

_____

_____

_____

_____

_____

_____

I love my unique attributes. (Identify each attribute and why you love it.)

_____

_____

_____

_____

_____

_____

Pursue Confidently

You are the Designer's original. Establish your goal.

In the next year, with the knowledge that I am the Designer's original, my goal is to:

_____

_____

_____

_____

_____

_____

Latasha G. Hines, Esq.

Write to your future self. Remind yourself that you are the Designer's original.

Here I am. It's ___ a.m./p.m. on _____, 20__. Today, I have been reminded that I am the Designer's original. Knowing this causes me to feel _____ _____ and empowers me to _____.

At this stage of my journey, I am working toward my goal by _____ _____.

One year from now, I want to remind myself that _____ _____.

I want to encourage my future self to keep pursuing my goal with confidence because _____ _____.

Latasha G. Hines, Esq.

Session 2

You Are a Gift

Not only are you the Designer's original, you are a precious gift. Of the approximately 100 million sperm released into your mother's womb, one sperm found an egg that existed in your mother's ovary since she was born. Then, there was the struggle to find just the right spot to implant and make a home for the next 10 weeks.

Of the 6 million women who get pregnant each year, only 4 million of the pregnancies result in a live birth. (www.pregnancystatistics.org, 02 Apr. 2015) Indeed, your very arrival into this world is a gift. The circumstance of your arrival may have been challenging. But, what matters is that you survived. There is purpose behind your survival. Pursue, knowing that you are a survivor.

You, the precious gift, have gifts to share with others. Someone is waiting on your gift to make a difference in their life. Perhaps it's the book you must write, the dress you long to design, the professional license you yearn to obtain, the doll you must create, the invention you must patent, the song you must sing, the speech you must give, the lesson you must share, or a number of other things.

Pursue Confidently

Not only are you a gift, but you have gifts and talents to share with others. Allow knowing this to propel you to pursue confidently.

I am thankful for the gift I received one summer afternoon from a man who pursued and accomplished his goal of becoming a life guard. My daughter, Mikayla, along with a group of other four and five-year-old children were taking swimming lessons at our community pool. As usual, I sat near the pool watching my daughter during the class. She hung on the edge, waiting for her turn with the instructor who took each student out to the middle of the pool and taught them to paddle back to the edge using a flotation device. *Easy enough*, I thought.

A fellow mom asked me a question about the zoo. I turned to respond to her. At some point during my response, I heard a whistle blow. I turned just in time to see the life guard jump into the water. I looked to the edge of the pool where the children had been hanging on as they waited for the instructor. I did not see Mikayla. In what seemed like minutes, although I am sure it was only seconds, I saw the lifeguard emerge from the water with Mikayla in his arm. Although she had taken in some water, she was fine. I had been given a gift from someone who pursued his goal and became a lifeguard.

The life guard acknowledged, only once, my many, many thank you cries. He then waived me off and took his post at the next life guard station. He probably felt like he was just doing his job. The fact that he did his job that day was a gift to me.

Do not judge the gift I received in context with the goal you are pursuing. It's all about perspective. For me, this was a life-changing moment, one of the greatest gifts I have ever received. Not all gifts involve such valiant efforts. I have heard many stories of people who received the gift of a smile that gave them strength to live another day. I have been on the receiving end of encouraging words that propelled me to keep keepin' on.

Prepare to be a gift who shares your gifts with others.

Pursue Confidently

You are a precious gift with talents to share. Reflect on the following and write your thoughts.

I am a precious gift.

_____

_____

_____

_____

_____

_____

I have special talents and skills to offer as gifts to others. (Identify your talents and skills and explain how you can use them to help others.)

_____

_____

_____

_____

_____

_____

Although I have many talents and skills, I believe my greatest talent or skill is the following: (Identify your greatest talent or skill and explain why you believe it is your greatest.)

_____

_____

_____

_____

_____

You are a precious gift with talents to share. Establish your goal.

In the next year, with the knowledge that I am a precious gift with talents to share with others, my goal is to:

_____

_____

_____

_____

Pursue Confidently

Write to your future self. Remind yourself that you are a precious gift with talents to share.

Here I am. It's ___ a.m./p.m. on _____, 20__. Today, I have been reminded that I am a precious gift with talents to share. Knowing this makes me feel _____ _____ and empowers me to _____.

At this stage of my journey, I am working toward my goal by _____

_____.

One year from now, I want to remind myself that

_____

_____.

I want to encourage my future self to keep pressing forward because _____

_____.

Latasha G. Hines, Esq.

Session 3

You Are Equipped

Whatever your goal is, life experiences have equipped you to pursue that goal. We learn throughout our life journey as we experience the joys of victories, agonies of defeats, satisfactions of successes, and disappointments of failures.

Victories have taught me that despite how challenging something can be, hard work ultimately pays off. Law school was a great challenge for me. There were no lawyers in my family and I did not know any personally. However, having earned the opportunity to go to law school, I knew I would have to work extra hard to complete law school successfully. I did just that. I studied excessively earning me the superlative title of "Most Likely to Pitch a Tent in the Library." I graduated with honors.

Disappointments in relationships have taught me to love myself and trust God above all others. Through failed relationships I have learned that people are fallible. But, my God is always there for me and supplies all that I need. (Deuteronomy 31:8; Philippians 4:14.) These experiences have equipped me with perseverance to push past disappointments. What have disappointments taught you?

Pursue Confidently

For some goals, a college degree, a technical class, or an instructional course may be required. If so, pursue it. Even so, educational training alone does not dictate whether you are equipped to pursue your goal. Life has equipped you for some stages of the pursuit of your goal.

Many of us have had experiences in this life that cause us to question whether we "have what it takes." However, the very things that have challenged your confidence are the very things that have equipped you to pursue your goal. Begin with what you have. Then, pursue what you need to accomplish your goal.

My grandparents lived in the James E. Scott housing projects in Liberty City in Miami, Florida. They helped to raise my cousins and me there. They did not have much but I learned a lot growing up, both good and bad.

My grandmother, Bessie Mae Clark, taught me to fight. She fought for me at school, where she insisted that I be placed in advanced classes. She fought for me at the local clinic, where she insisted that I receive better medical care to address my severe childhood asthma. She drove me to neighborhoods far from where we lived so that I could compete in oratorical contests. She learned my speeches so that I could look to her as a source of comfort whenever I forgot a part of my speech.

She fought for me with what she had—her voice and her love for me. She could have resolved that we did not have significant means and that I would not rise above our circumstances. Thankfully, she did not. She used what she had to fight for what I needed to have a chance to succeed. Then, she sought the help of others to help me along the way. She did not allow lack to rob me of opportunities to excel. Her loving support equipped me to pursue my goals with confidence.

And for those who questioned whether something good could come out of the James E. Scott housing projects, the answer is "yes." Among Mrs. Bessie's grandchildren are educators, engineers, a lawyer, a PhD candidate, a published author, and a detective. The good and bad of our environment equipped us to excel.

In Napoleon Hill's book, *Think and Grow Rich*, he writes: "Every adversity, every failure, and every heartache carries with it the Seed of an equivalent or greater Benefit (or Blessing)". Will you allow your adversities, failures, and heartaches to birth something greater?

Stop beating yourself up for the failures, the missed steps, and the harm inflicted by others. You—the Designer's original, the gift—must love you first. As you embrace your love for you, you will be empowered to pursue your goal with full assurance that you've earned some degrees from the School of Life to help propel you toward your goal.

You are equipped to pursue your goal. Reflect on the following and write your thoughts.

I am equipped to pursue my goal.

_____

_____

_____

_____

_____

_____

I will use the following positive life experiences to help me pursue my goal:

(Identify positive life experiences that have equipped you to pursue your goal.)

_____

_____

_____

_____

_____

_____

I will use the following negative life experiences to help me pursue my goal:

(Identify negative life experiences that have equipped you to pursue your goal.)

_____

_____

_____

_____

_____

You are equipped to pursue your goal. Establish your goal.

In the next year, with the knowledge that I am equipped to pursue my goal, my goal is to:

_____

_____

_____

_____

_____

_____

Pursue Confidently

Write to your future self. Remind yourself that you are equipped to pursue your goal.

Here I am. It's ___ a.m./p.m. on _____, 20__. Today, I have been reminded that I am equipped to pursue my goal. Knowing this makes me feel _____ and empowers me to _____

_____.

At this stage of my journey, I am working toward my goal by _____

_____.

One year from now, I want to remind myself that

_____

_____.

I want to encourage my future self to keep pressing forward because _____

_____.

Session 4

Activate Your Plan
(Apply Sessions 1 – 3)

You, the Designer's original and precious gift, are equipped to pursue your goal.

Today, knowing that I am the Designer's original and a precious gift who is equipped to pursue my goal, I will take the following steps toward achieving my goal:

_____

_____

_____

This month, knowing that I am the Designer's original and a precious gift who is equipped to pursue my goal, I will take the following steps toward achieving my goal:

_____

_____

_____

Pursue Confidently

By the end of the next six months, knowing that I am the Designer's original and a precious gift who is equipped to pursue my goal, I will take the following steps toward achieving my goal:

_____

_____

_____

By the end of this year, knowing that I am the Designer's original and a precious gift who is equipped to pursue my goal, I will have:

_____

_____

_____

Part II

Be Confident; Embrace Healthy Relationships

Why are we addressing relationships in the context of a book on confidently pursing your goals? Relationships play a key role in pursuing your goals with confidence. A healthy relationship propels you toward your goal. An unhealthy relationship can propel you away from your goal.

As you prepare to pursue your goal with confidence, you must assess the relationships that impact you the most. Typically, the relationships that impact us the most are those with spouses or significant others, family members, and business associates.

When I am at peace in these various relationships, I experience greater mental freedom to pursue my goals. Loving and nurturing environments provide a safety net that gives me freedom to launch out, knowing that others will be there for me whether I excel or experience temporary failure.

There are times, however, that even in the absence of such peace, I am compelled to pursue my goals. There are times when working through tough relationships require substantial time. Yet, we cannot always delay the pursuit of our goal as we try to resolve relationship issues. While the challenges of the relationship may make the pursuit more difficult, perhaps slowing the pursuit, you must pursue nevertheless.

Healthy relationships include give and take. There may not be an equal amount of give and take, but you must give and receive in a relationship. (Session 6) Indeed love gives, endures, trusts, perseveres, protects, and keeps no record of wrong. (I Corinthians 13:4-7.) Extending love is rewarding as you embrace the love of yourself and share the gift of you with others. (Session 5) Love reciprocated is also rewarding and empowering. When you are healthy, you are able to establish boundaries that compel healthy relationships with spouses or significant others, family members, and business associates.

While it may be difficult to embrace this concept in the context of work environments, the principles remain the same. In the work environment, think about the love principles in the context of respect. Love is an "affection based on admiration, benevolence, or common interests." (*Merriam-Webster*. Web. 12 Apr. 2015.) Respect is a "high or special regard." (*Merriam-Webster*. Web. 02 Apr. 2015.) A healthy work relationship involves mutual respect.

The give and take of love is vital. Dr. Charles Stanley wrote, "If we never give it [love], we'll become self-centered and demanding. If we never receive it, we'll constantly strive for acceptance and approval." (In Touch Magazine, February 2015.) A measure of both give and take gives us the confidence required to pursue our goals.(Session 7)

You were designed to love and be loved. In this phase of the pursuit, we must embrace healthy relationships.

Latasha G. Hines, Esq.

Session 5

Created to Love Others

As you embrace self-love, you are empowered to love others. The love of your Creator flows out through you as you realize your value and the gifts you have to share with others.

Earlier, we embraced the fact that we are to love our neighbors as we love ourselves. Who is your neighbor? We share the earth with 7 billion people. It is easier to share our love with neighbors in our actual sphere of influence, such as our actual neighbors on the block, spouses, children, other family members, friends, and business associates to name a few.

However, the goals we pursue have the ability to impact far more than just the people in our sphere of influence. We will never know just how many people benefit from our love shared as our love shared with others empowers someone else to love another, and another, and another.

We are to love with the same measure of love we have for ourselves. When we are healthy, we are empowered to extend love wholeheartedly as we seek the best for others.

Pursue Confidently

The love you pour out to others strengthens you for your very own pursuit. You can pursue your goals with joy, knowing that your love makes a difference in the lives of others, whether they acknowledge it or not.

Indeed, there are those who we find very difficult to love because of harm they have inflicted, beliefs that cause and tolerate injustice, and disregard of others. Yet, we can extend love to that person, perhaps through a prayer, a thought, or a gesture, without subjecting ourselves to being harmed by them.

Lighten your load. Get rid of the baggage of anger and unforgiveness. Admittedly, forgiveness can be difficult. However, the pursuit of your goals depends on it. Love yourself enough to know when it's time to move on and when staying is worth the fight. Love others enough to know when to include them on your journey and when to let them go. You must not allow the wrongs of others to interfere with your confident pursuit of your goals. You have work to do, goals to accomplish. Allow love to propel you forward.

You were created to love others. Reflect on the following and write your thoughts.

My love helps others to/by: (Identify the effects of your love on others.)

_____

_____

_____

_____

_____

_____

When I express love to others, I express love for myself because I am giving an important part of me to others.

_____

_____

_____

_____

_____

Pursue Confidently

Loving _____ is difficult because

_____

_____

_____

However, I will extend love by:

_____

_____

_____

Latasha G. Hines, Esq.

You were created to love others. Establish your goal.

In the next year, with the knowledge that I was created to love, my goal is to:

_____

_____

_____

_____

_____

Pursue Confidently

Write to your future self. Remind yourself that you were created to love others.

Here I am. It's ___ a.m./p.m. on _____, 20__. Today, I have been reminded that I was created to love others. Knowing this makes me feel_____

and empowers me to _____

_____.

At this stage of my journey, I am working toward my goal by _____

_____.

One year from now, I want to remind myself that

_____

_____.

I want to encourage my future self to keep pressing forward because _____

_____.

Session 6

Worthy to Be Loved

As you embrace your value and the fact that you are to be an extension of love, you must understand that you are worthy to be loved. Often, it is easier to extend ourselves to others rather than love ourselves or encourage love from others. As a result, you can subject yourself to loveless relationships.

When you are healthy, you are able to establish boundaries that encourage a healthy relationship. Notice that I said "encourage". You cannot force a person to love or respect you. However, as you grasp that you are the Designer's original, a precious gift, you will act in a way that encourages others to honor the gift that you are. When someone does not honor you as the gift that you are, you will have the confidence to protect yourself from mistreatment, refusing to settle for less.

Unhealthy relationships can take you off track in the pursuit of your goal. If a person does not honor you as a gift, it can cause self-doubt, eroding the confidence to pursue your goal. Therefore, we must constantly evaluate the

Pursue Confidently

health of our relationships and use wisdom in making adjustments that empower us to pursue our goals. You will be empowered as you embrace the fact that the Designer took great care in creating a masterpiece—you. Then, be the gift that you are. Communicate your need to be loved and valued. Ultimately, seek wisdom in your relationships. Rise above the efforts of others to hinder your confident pursuit.

You are worthy to be loved. Reflect on the following and write your thoughts.

My relationship with _____

propels me toward my goal because:

_____

_____

_____

_____

My relationship with _____

hinders me from pursuing my goal; therefore, I will make the following changes:

_____

_____

_____

_____

Pursue Confidently

You are worthy to be loved. Establish your goal.

In the next year, with the knowledge that I am worthy to be loved, my goal is to:

_____

_____

_____

_____

_____

_____

Latasha G. Hines, Esq.

Write to your future self. Remind yourself that you are worthy to be loved.

Here I am. It's ___ a.m./p.m. on _____, 20__. Today, I have been reminded that I am worthy to be loved. Knowing this makes me feel_____ and empowers me to _____ _____.

At this stage of my journey, I am working toward my goal by _____ _____.

One year from now, I want to remind myself that _____ _____.

I want to encourage my future self to keep pressing forward because _____ _____.

Session 7

Love Confidently

Some may wonder why there has been a great focus on love in the context of a book aimed to empower the reader to confidently pursue their goals. I believe that love is one of the greatest forces in the universe. The presence or absence of love impacts our lives in profound ways. We must address the issues of love of self and others in preparation for the pursuit of our goals.

Our love for others is an extension of the love we have from the Designer. We can love others confidently, knowing that we have the greatest love of all from the Designer who knit us together and presented us as gifts to the world.

Relationships have given many of us bumps and bruises along the way. We cannot allow those challenges to strip us of who we are. Relationships have empowered us to aim high and excel in aspects of life. The joy and comfort of love received gives us the strength to pursue. We have the ability to offer such love to others.

Pursue Confidently

To love confidently is to extend love and receive love, knowing that you are a precious gift whether others embrace you as a gift or not. Love releases you from the burdens of others. Peace comes with knowing that you have extended yourself for the good of someone else.

Latasha G. Hines, Esq.

You must love confidently. Reflect on the following and write your thoughts.

I am empowered when I extend love to others, even when they don't deserve my love:

_____
_____
_____
_____
_____
_____

I can confidently extend love to others because I love me.

_____
_____
_____
_____
_____
_____

Pursue Confidently

You will love confidently. Establish your goal.

In the next year, with the knowledge that I must love confidently, my goal is to:

_____

_____

_____

_____

_____

_____

Latasha G. Hines, Esq.

Write to your future self. Remind yourself that you will love confidently.

Here I am. It's ___ a.m./p.m. on _____, 20__. Today, I have been empowered to love confidently. Knowing this makes me feel_____ and empowers me to _____ _____.

At this stage of my journey, I am working toward my goal by _____ _____.

One year from now, I want to remind myself that _____ _____.

I want to encourage my future self to keep pressing forward because _____ _____.

Session 8

Activate Your Plan
(Apply Sessions 5 – 7)

Love confidently, recognizing that you were created to love and be loved.

Today, with the knowledge that I must love confidently, I will take the following steps toward achieving my goal:

_____

_____

_____

This month, with the knowledge that I must love confidently, I will take the following steps toward achieving my goal:

_____

_____

_____

Pursue Confidently

By the end of the next six months, with the knowledge that I must love confidently, I will take the following steps toward achieving my goal:

_____

_____

_____

By the end of this year, with the knowledge that I must love confidently, I will have:

_____

_____

_____

Part III

Be Confident; Pursue Your Goals

There is victory in beginning the pursuit. Often, beginning is the toughest part of the journey. Some never make the attempt. Their goal remains tucked away in the security of their inner thoughts, secure from judgment from others. They don't risk the negative talk of the doubters or the challenging questions of the encourager. They get stuck questioning whether to give voice to their dreams.

The ideas form a whirlwind in their head. Does my idea make sense? Can I really make it happen? How can I afford to pursue it? What will others think? Press past the questions and begin your pursuit now. (Session 9)

It is time to move those thoughts to paper. Write them out. Don't try to make them all make sense as you write. Just write. Deposit all of your thoughts onto paper. There will come a time to give them more focus or craft them more concisely. But for now, just write them all down.

Pursue Confidently

Give voice to those thoughts by speaking them aloud to yourself and to others. Stand in a mirror and speak your ideas to yourself. Tell yourself why you must accomplish your goals and how others will be blessed by what you have to share.

Tell a friend or even a stranger about your goals and how you plan to accomplish them. Solicit their thoughts and suggestions. Be prepared to weigh the advice and responses, tossing the bad and embracing the useful.

Pursue your goal with excellence, pouring in all that you have to give. Be wise enough to seek the help of others as you pursue your goal. (Session 10) And, sometimes you must pursue even when fear is trailing you. (Session 11)

You must begin the pursuit. Let us prepare to pursue with urgency, excellence, and confidence.

Latasha G. Hines, Esq.

Session 9

Pursue with Urgency

You must prepare now. Now is the time to pursue your goal with urgency. Perhaps you have dreamed of accomplishing your goal for many years. Perhaps you have a goal that originated when you were a child. Your goal could have taken root just last week or even today. Whatever you dream of accomplishing and whenever the idea entered your thought and your heart, you must act now. Take steps to bring that dream to past. Pursue urgently because so much and so many are counting on the gift you have to share.

Self-fulfillment awaits you as you take the steps necessary to pursue and accomplish goal. With each accomplished goal, your confidence to excel in other aspects of life will grow. You will have the confidence of knowing that you can accomplish your goals once you apply yourself. As you persevere to share your gift with others, you are strengthened to strengthen others to do the same.

There is another reason you must pursue your goal with urgency. You are mortal. Surely, you will die. Time is precious. We do not know the amount of time we have left in the earth. I pray that at the stage you read this book, you have a long, healthy, and prosperous life ahead of you. Even so, do not procrastinate.

As a lawyer, I have counseled clients in basic estate planning. Typically, it takes a client a year from the time they initially contact me to the time we formalize an estate plan, and often it takes even longer. Generally, clients struggle with the details. Should I sell the investment property before I die and give the money to children in equal distributions now? Or, should I give my child Bill 45% because he has helped me financially when I needed it over the years, give my child Susan 35% because she is a single parent who needs help supporting her children, and give my child Derrick 10% so that I don't make him mad although he never calls or visits me. (The names are fictional.)

The client wants to give something to their children. They have no problem listing their names on the questionnaire. They know they can make changes later. However, they struggle with the details of the percentages and the reasons behind those percentages, so much so that sometimes they never execute an estate plan prior to death. Then, the laws of the state determine how their estate is distributed.

Do not take your gifts to the grave. Prepare to leave them here to bless others. There are many children enjoying the benefits of songs recorded by their uncle, music composed by their father, books written by their mother, ideas patented by their grandfather, and lessons taught by their teachers. They now enjoy these benefits because someone pursued and accomplished their goal prior to death.

Pursue with urgency the goals you have established.

Pursue your goal with urgency. Reflect on the following and write your thoughts.

If I restructure the following aspects of my life, I will have more time to pursue my goal.

_____

_____

_____

_____

_____

_____

If I die without accomplishing my goal, others will never experience my gift.

_____

_____

_____

_____

_____

_____

Pursue Confidently

Describe a time you had an all-nighter, meaning you stayed up for 24 hours. Was it to prepare for a test? Were you enjoying an activity? Are you willing to give up sleep to jumpstart or propel your goal?

_____

_____

_____

_____

_____

Urgently pursue your goal. Establish your goal.

In the next year, with the knowledge that I must pursue my goal with urgency, my goal is to:

_____

_____

_____

_____

_____

Latasha G. Hines, Esq.

Write to your future self. Remind yourself that you will pursue your goal with urgency.

Here I am. It's ___ a.m./p.m. on _____, 20__. Today, I embrace the fact that I should pursue my goal with urgency. Knowing this makes me feel_____

_____ and empowers me to

_____.

At this stage of my journey, I am working toward my goal by _____

_____.

One year from now, I want to remind myself that

_____

_____.

I want to encourage my future self to keep pressing forward because _____

_____.

Latasha G. Hines, Esq.

Session 10

Pursue with Excellence

Not only is it time for you to do it—whatever your "it" is—but you must do it with excellence. As you pursue your goal, do your very best. Pour out your skills, training, education, gifts, life experiences, and common sense to do your very, very best. Give it your all. Do not compromise.

Recognize your weaknesses. Pursuing with excellence does not mean that you have all the tools to accomplish your goal. A part of pursuing with excellence is recognizing when you need the help of others. While many of us are multi-talented and have great contributions to make toward the goals we pursue, we will need help to ensure excellence.

It took me five years to write my first book, *I Love Him Lord,® but He's Not a Christian: The Christian Woman's Guide to Deliverance from Toxic Relationships*. While I relied on the skills learned as a journalism student and journalist, I tried to be the copy editor and book designer although I didn't have adequate skills. My first book was "my baby" and I was set on doing it my way. It was a good first effort, but it was not excellent.

Pursue Confidently

A year later, I release a revised edition of the book after employing the help of a professional editor, artist, and book designer to help make my book excellent. If I had reached out for help sooner, I could have given my gift to the world sooner. I have met people and received letters and emails from people who were empowered to avoid or get out of toxic relationships after reading my book. I wish I understood in the initial stages that I could have arrived at excellence a lot sooner.

Confidently pursue your goals by giving your best efforts and seeking the help of others to help with your weaknesses.

You will pursue your goal with excellence. Reflect on the following and write your thoughts.

I have training, skills, talents, and abilities to pursue my goal with excellence. (Identify them specifically.)

_____

_____

_____

_____

_____

I need others to help me pursue my goal with excellence. (Identify the type of help you need.)

_____

_____

_____

_____

_____

Pursue Confidently

I will pursue my goal with excellence. Establish your goal.

In the next year, with the knowledge that I will pursue my goal with excellence, my goal is to:

_____

_____

_____

_____

_____

Latasha G. Hines, Esq.

Write to your future self. Remind yourself that you will pursue your goal with excellence.

Here I am. It's ___ a.m./p.m. on _____, 20__. Today, I have been empowered to pursue my goal with excellence. Knowing this makes me feel_____ and empowers me to _____

_____.

At this stage of my journey, I am working toward my goal by _____

_____.

One year from now, I want to remind myself that

_____

_____.

I want to encourage my future self to keep pressing forward because _____

_____.

Latasha G. Hines, Esq.

Session 11

Pursue Confidently

The cheetah is a master hunter in the animal kingdom, known for his pursuit. The cheetah uses his keen eyesight to plan its pursuit. (*Cheetah,* www.nationalgeographics.com, 03 Apr. 2015.) Often, he spots his prey in the distance. The cheetah understands that the day's meal requires it to pursue, even if there is a significant distance between him and his prey.

Some of your goals may seem far away. Perhaps you struggle with how you will make that goal a reality. Are my finances sufficient? Do I have enough time? What will others think and say? How do I actually do it? While these are important issues to consider, do not allow these issues to stop you from beginning the pursuit. Each step you take moves you toward your goal. You will find that once you are in motion, the answers and opportunities come. The key is to make a plan, then pursue.

The cheetah factors in his strengths and weaknesses. Speed is his strength. He is weak at fighting off scavengers after he makes the kill. Therefore, he often drags his kill

Pursue Confidently

to a shady area to protect it from other animals. (Ibid.) Like the cheetah, use your strengths to begin the pursuit and make adjustments based on your weaknesses.

Pursue confidently, knowing that your strengths will take you a great distance and that the strengths of others will help you accomplish your goals. Although others may help you with aspects of your goal, it remains *your* goal to accomplish.

Fear may rise up to thwart your confident pursuit of your goal. Recognize fear for what it is—an anxious concern—but resolve that you will pursue nevertheless. If fear wants to hang around and tug on you, let it. But let it do so with purpose. If you must deal with it, use fear to propel you toward your goal.

Three years ago, I prepared to argue before a three-judge panel at the State of Florida Third District Court of Appeal for the very first time. During my years of legal practice I had become accustomed to arguing my client's position before a single judge. Now it was time to face three appellate court judges and convince them that the trial court judge made the right decision.

I had a lot of restless nights as I prepared. I dedicated a lot of time reviewing the details of the case and the relevant case law. It was not enough to give me peace. I sought out the counsel of a trusted colleague and friend who helped me prepare and gain the confidence I needed to pursue this goal of arguing before an appellate court.

I acknowledged the fear that hung out with me until the moment I stood before the panel of judges and announced my name. Nevertheless, I pressed pass fear and made my arguments to three judges. Indeed, this was a three-judge panel but ultimately the rules of engagement were the same. I had to plan my pursuit, then pursue with confidence relying on my faith, my skills and the help of my colleague.

What must you confidently pursue?

Pursue Confidently

You have the confidence to pursue your goal. Reflect on the following and write your thoughts.

I am frightened by the following aspects of pursuing my goal. Nevertheless, I will pursue it, even if it means doing it afraid.

_____
_____
_____
_____
_____
_____

As I pursue my goal, the one thing I am confident of is:

_____
_____
_____
_____
_____
_____

Latasha G. Hines, Esq.

You have the confidence to pursue your goal. Establish your goal.

In the next year, with the knowledge that I have the confidence to pursue my goal, my goal is to:

_____

_____

_____

_____

_____

_____

Pursue Confidently

Write to your future self. Remind yourself that you can pursue your goal with confidence.

Here I am. It's ___ a.m./p.m. on _____, 20__. Today, I have been reminded that I can and will pursue my goal with confidence. Knowing this makes me feel _____ and empowers me to _____.

At this stage of my journey, I am working toward my goal by _____

_____.

One year from now, I want to remind myself that

_____

_____.

I want to encourage my future self to keep pressing forward because _____

_____.

Session 12

Activate Your Plan
(Apply Sessions 9 – 11)

Pursue your goal with urgency, excellence, and confidence.

Today, committed to pursue my goal with urgency, excellence, and confidence, I will take the following steps toward achieving my goal:

_____

_____

_____

This month, committed to pursue my goal with urgency, excellence, and confidence, I will take the following steps toward achieving my goal:

_____

_____

_____

Pursue Confidently

By the end of the next six months, committed to pursue my goal with urgency, excellence, and confidence, I will take the following steps toward achieving my goal:

_____

_____

_____

By the end of this year, committed to pursue my goal with urgency, excellence, and confidence, I will have:

_____

_____

_____

Conclusion

Pursue Confidently has been your guide through sessions designed to help you embrace your value and pursue your goals. The pursuit begins with a plan. Through these exercises you have reflected on matters of the heart that may have impacted your ability to confidently pursue your goals in the past, established or refined your current goals, and made a plan to pursue those goals.

The pursuit is underway. Continue to make the efforts necessary to achieve your goals. Pursue with a renewed love for the Designer's masterpiece—you. Pursue with a renewed commitment to embracing healthy relationships. Pursue your goals with confidence, knowing that you are indeed equipped for the pursuit.

About the Author

Latasha Gethers Hines, Esq. is a writer, speaker, and teacher who empowers others to embrace an abundant life and use their talents to bless others and the Kingdom of God. Latasha shares powerful message with book clubs, civic groups, Bible study groups, churches, businesses, and in empowerment sessions.

She is a multi-faceted business woman who, along with her husband, owns Jewel Publishers, LLC of which Latasha Hines Speaks is a division. She is a successful business consultant and attorney who represents corporations and individuals in business matters.

In 1994, Latasha earned a Bachelor of Science degree in journalism and a minor in speech communication from the University of Florida where she was inducted into the Student Hall of Fame. She earned a Juris Doctor degree in 1997 from the University of Miami School of Law, where she graduated *cum laude*.

A Miami-native, Latasha lives in South Florida with her husband, Travis, and their children, Mikayla and Matthew. She has a step-daughter, Teylor.

Latasha is the author of the *I Love Him Lord®* series which includes *I Love Him Lord®, but He's Not a Christian: The Christian Woman's Guide to Deliverance from Toxic Relationships* and the upcoming book, *I Love Him Lord, Now Teach Me to Respect Him: A Guide to Love and Marriage*.

Purchase *Pursue Confidently* at bookstores, www.amazon.com, www.jewelpublishers.com, or anywhere books are sold.

Contact us for discounted book rates for orders of 10 books or more.

Jewel Publishers, LLC
P. O. Box 278006
Miramar, FL 33027
www.jewelpublishers.com
admin@jewelpublishers.com

Latasha G. Hines, Esq.
Speaking Engagement Inquiry Form

Use this convenient form to inquire about Latasha G. Hines' availability to speak to groups including civic, charitable, and professional organizations.

Please Print:

Name_____

Address_____

City_____ State _____ Zip_____

Phone_____

Proposed Date and Time _____

Event _____

Theme _____

Program Format _____

_____

Comments _____

_____

Jewel Publishers, LLC
P. O. Box 278006
Miramar, FL 33027
www.jewelpublishers.com
admin@jewelpublishers.com

www.ingramcontent.com/pod-product-compliance
Lightning Source LLC
Chambersburg PA
CBHW071457070426
42452CB00040B/1550